Curious Histories:
Fascinating Tales They Never Taught You in School

Curious Mind Series (Book I)

Curious Histories: Fascinating Tales They Never Taught You in School

Curious Mind Series, Book I

Contents

Introduction – Welcome to the Weird Side of History

Where kings stumble, disasters get sticky, and humans do the most ridiculous things imaginable.

Hello there, curious reader!

If you picked up this book expecting neat rows of kings, queens, and endless battles with lots of boring dates, well... you're in for a *pleasant surprise*. Because history, as it turns out, isn't just pomp, parades, and politics. No, no. It's way messier. Way funnier. Way stickier (and sometimes smellier) than anyone ever told you in school.

History is:

I.   **Accidents that changed the world** – like a molasses flood that drowned an entire city block.

II. **Humans behaving strangely** – ever hear of people dancing themselves to death in 1518?

III. **Brilliant ideas born from messes** – penicillin, anyone?

IV. **Coincidences that make you go "Wait, what?!"** – twins, disasters, and strangely timed inventions.

- And, of course, **plenty of moments that just make you shake your head** and whisper, "Humans are ridiculous."

We're not just here to recount wars, treaties, and political intrigue. Nope. This book is a guided tour of history's **odder side**, where mistakes become miracles, boredom sparks epidemics, and ordinary people accidentally shape the future in ways even the textbooks can't handle.

Every story in these pages is **100% true**, and every one of them is probably **stranger than fiction**. You'll meet people whose ideas were brilliant, bizarre, or completely baffling. You'll see disasters that should have never happened — and in some cases, still can't be believed. And, hopefully, you'll laugh, gasp, and maybe even tell your friends, "Did you know *this actually happened?*"

So grab your favorite beverage, get comfortable, and prepare to step into the **weird, wonderful, and absolutely unpredictable world of history**.

Trust me — once you start, you'll never look at the past the same way again.

Part I – Accidents That Changed Everything

Short, fascinating tales of lucky mistakes, flukes, and unintended inventions.

1. **The Great Molasses Flood of 1919** – *when Boston drowned in syrup.*

2. **Penicillin and the Messy Desk** – *how a dirty Petri dish changed medicine.*

3. **The Discovery of X-Rays** – *a glowing screen and a shocked scientist.*

4. **The Potato Chip Revolution** – *one angry chef and a picky customer.*

5. **Coca-Cola's Accidental Invention** – *from headache tonic to global brand.*

ONE

1. The Great Molasses Flood of 1919

When Boston got stuck in a very sticky situation.

On a crisp January afternoon in 1919, Bostonians were minding their own business — probably walking around in heavy wool coats, grumbling about the cold, and wondering why tea hadn't fixed all of life's problems yet — when *it* happened.

A **massive storage tank filled with 2.3 million gallons of molasses** (that's enough syrup to drown a city block in pancakes) suddenly burst open like an overripe water balloon.

Within seconds, a **25-foot-high wall of sticky brown goo** came roaring through Boston's North End. The wave traveled at **35 miles per hour**, which is a terrifying speed for something usually seen dribbling lazily out of a bottle.

Horses, carts, and entire buildings were swept up in the sugary tsunami. People tried to run, but — and this will surprise no one — **it's hard to sprint through molasses**. When it finally stopped, the neighborhood looked like Willy Wonka's factory had exploded.

Cleanup took weeks. The smell lingered for decades. (Locals swore you could still catch a whiff of molasses on hot days even into the 1960s.)

Fun Fact

Molasses moves faster when it's warm — and that day, an unseasonably warm snap had thinned the syrup just enough to make it deadly. Basically, the weather turned Boston into a dessert topping.

The Sticky Science Bit

Molasses, or "black treacle" if you're feeling fancy, is a byproduct of sugar refining. When the tank burst, the pressure change caused **a shockwave** that literally blew the steel apart. Witnesses said the ground "shook like an earthquake," and engineers later blamed poor construction and neglect.

Translation: someone didn't do their maintenance.

Did You Know?

The company responsible — the Purity Distilling Company — tried to blame "anarchists" for blowing up the tank. Turns out it was just physics and bad welding.

TWO

2. Penicillin and the Messy Desk

When one sloppy scientist changed medicine forever.

In 1928, **Alexander Fleming** was the kind of scientist who could turn forgetfulness into a world-changing discovery. His lab was... let's say, "messy." Petri dishes stacked haphazardly, papers everywhere, the occasional suspicious smell — basically your teenage bedroom, but with germs.

One fateful day, Fleming noticed that a mold called **Penicillium notatum** had accidentally contaminated one of his Staphylococcus bacterial cultures. Most people would throw it away and mutter, *"Ugh, clean your desk!"*

But not Fleming. He squinted at the moldy dish and realized: **this mold was killing bacteria.**

Boom. Penicillin. The first true antibiotic. Thousands of lives would later be saved, all thanks to one messy desk and a scientist who didn't hate fungi.

Fun Fact

Fleming didn't immediately mass-produce penicillin. That honor went to others in the 1940s — so in a way, he discovered it, and someone else got the party started.

THREE

3. The Discovery of X-Rays

A glowing screen and a shocked scientist.

It's **late 1895**, in a dark, cluttered laboratory in Würzburg, Germany. **Wilhelm Conrad Röntgen** is tinkering with a cathode ray tube — basically a glass tube with wires sticking out of it — while muttering to himself and probably wishing for a stronger cup of coffee.

He's not trying to change the world. He's not even trying to see inside people. He's just a scientist doing his thing, like any curious nerd in a lab would. But then something bizarre happens.

A **fluorescent screen across the room starts glowing** — and it's not supposed to. The room is dark, the tube is sealed, and yet the screen lights up like a miniature sun. Röntgen, ever the careful observer, decides to investigate. He waves his hand in front of the screen... and sees something shocking.

He sees **his own bones**. Right there, floating in a ghostly glow against the black background. His fingers are clearly visible, each phalange outlined like the world's creepiest shadow puppet.

At first, Röntgen probably blinked. And then he laughed. Or maybe gasped. Or both. Whatever he did, he realized **he had just discovered something incredible**: a way to see inside living beings without cutting them open.

Fun Fact

Röntgen called them **"X-rays"** because X = unknown (math nerd alert). And yes, the "X" stuck. He had no idea just how famous and useful this accidental discovery would become.

The Science Bit

- X-rays are a form of **electromagnetic radiation** — like light, but sneaky.

- They pass through soft tissue but bounce off dense matter like bones.

- This property lets us see inside the body safely (well, mostly safely — early radiologists got a lot of burns).

So basically, Röntgen created the ultimate backstage pass for the human body. No scalpel required.

Did You Know?

- Röntgen didn't patent X-rays. He believed knowledge should be shared freely. Imagine discovering a technology that would save millions of lives and just giving it away. Talk about generosity.

- He also took the **first X-ray of his wife's hand** — her skeleton became the world's first X-ray celebrity.

FOUR

4. The Potato Chip Revolution

One angry chef and a picky customer.

It all began with a tantrum.

Not the kind where a toddler screams because their sandwich was cut into triangles instead of squares — no, this was an *adult tantrum*. A culinary standoff that would end up changing snack history forever.

The year was **1853**. The place: **Moon's Lake House**, a fashionable resort restaurant in Saratoga Springs, New York — a place where rich folks came to "take the waters," gossip about each other, and enjoy fancy dinners.

In the kitchen, a man named **George Crum** was running things. Crum was known for his excellent cooking, his sharp knives, and his even sharper attitude when dealing with rude customers.

And one day, in walked *that* customer.

Enter the Picky Eater

The story goes that a wealthy diner (some say it was railroad magnate Cornelius Vanderbilt himself —

history's not sure, but it sounds deliciously dramatic) ordered fried potatoes.

Simple enough, right? Crum made them, sent them out... and a few minutes later, the waiter came back with the plate.

"The gentleman says the potatoes are too thick," the waiter mumbled.

Crum frowned. "Too thick?" he repeated, probably holding a knife in a way that made the waiter take a careful step back.

Fine. He'd slice them thinner.

He did. Fried them again. Salted them perfectly. Sent them out.

Moments later: the plate came back. "The gentleman says they're still too thick."

Crum's patience snapped like a dry breadstick.

Petty Genius

With a combination of rage and genius, Crum decided to *teach this customer a lesson*. He sliced the potatoes **so thin you could practically read a newspaper through them**. He fried them until they were **crispy and golden brown**, the oil sizzling with culinary vengeance.

Then — and this part's important — he **salted the life out of them**.

He sent the plate back out, ready to smirk when the customer inevitably choked on his own snobbery.

Except... the man loved them.

In fact, he *raved* about them. He said they were the best thing he'd ever eaten. And then, of course, all the other rich guests wanted to try them too.

Crum had just invented the **potato chip** — or as they were called back then, **Saratoga Chips**.

A Crunch Heard Round the World

Word spread quickly. People couldn't get enough of the crisp, salty, paper-thin marvels.

Crum's "revenge snack" became the restaurant's most famous dish. Eventually, he opened his own establishment, where every table featured a basket of chips.

They weren't just a side dish anymore — they were the *main attraction*.

But Crum never patented the recipe. Like many of history's great accidental geniuses, he didn't realize his creation would conquer the globe one crunch at a time.

Fun Fact:

When potato chips first became popular, they were considered **fancy food** — served in high-end hotels and restaurants. It wasn't until the 1920s that industrial packaging turned them into a snack for the masses. Before that, chips were so posh they could have come with monocles.

The Science of the Crunch

Let's talk physics (just a little — no homework, promise).

What makes potato chips *so* addictive?

- **Surface area** – By slicing potatoes thin, Crum maximized the crispy outer layer.

- **Moisture reduction** – Frying drives out water, creating that satisfying crunch.

- **Salt** – Not only enhances flavor but literally triggers dopamine in your brain. (Translation: your brain loves salt almost as much as it loves gossip.)

It's chemistry, physics, and emotional therapy all rolled into one bite.

The Snack Revolution

By the early 20th century, potato chips had escaped the fancy resorts and invaded lunchboxes everywhere. In 1926, a woman named **Laura Scudder** revolutionized the chip world again by **packing them in wax paper bags** — keeping them fresh and crispy for days.

No more soggy snacks. No more heartbreak.

A few decades later, big brands like Lay's industrialized the process, flavoring chips with everything from barbecue spice to... prawn cocktail (which, depending on who you ask, was either progress or a culinary crime).

FIVE

5. Coca-Cola's Accidental Invention

From headache tonic to global brand.

Picture this: **Atlanta, Georgia, 1886.**

The air is thick, the heat relentless, and inside a small pharmacy called **Jacobs' Drug Store**, a man named **Dr. John Stith Pemberton** is cooking up what he swears will be the next big thing in medicine.

Pemberton isn't your average pharmacist. He's part doctor, part inventor, part mad scientist. He wears spectacles, probably mutters to himself while stirring concoctions, and definitely smells faintly of menthol and ambition.

You see, Pemberton had a problem. During the American Civil War, he'd been injured and became addicted to **morphine**, which was basically 19th-century pain relief that worked *too well*. He wanted a cure — not just for his addiction, but for the headaches, fatigue, and general misery of modern life.

So, like any respectable inventor, he decided to create his own medicine.

And that medicine would accidentally become **Coca-Cola.**

The Magic Recipe (Kind Of)

Pemberton's original formula was called **"Pemberton's French Wine Coca."**

Yes, *wine* — and *coca* — as in the coca leaf, the source of a certain infamous stimulant we won't name, but which starts with "C" and rhymes with *pocaine.*

Add a splash of kola nut extract (which contains caffeine), a drizzle of sugar syrup, and voila! You have a drink that's equal parts pick-me-up and party potion.

It was marketed as a cure for headaches, nervous disorders, and basically any ailment that wasn't fatal. (And maybe some that were.)

But then, in 1886, Atlanta decided to go **dry** — meaning alcohol was banned. Suddenly, "French Wine Coca" was about as legal as moonshine.

When Life Gives You Prohibition...

Rather than admit defeat, Pemberton did what all great inventors do when faced with disaster: he improvised.

He swapped the wine for **sugar syrup**, kept the coca leaf and kola nut, and added a hint of caramel color to make it look rich and appetizing.

He sent his assistant, **Frank Robinson**, to design a fancy logo (he's the one who came up with the name *Coca-Cola* and wrote it in that iconic cursive font).

Soon, the fizzy new drink was being served at soda fountains around Atlanta for **five cents a glass**.

People loved it. They said it made them feel "invigorated," "refreshed," and "strangely cheerful." No one could quite explain why. (Hint: *it still contained trace amounts of cocaine until 1904.*)

Fun Fact:

When Pemberton invented Coca-Cola, he had no idea what he'd unleashed. He sold the rights bit by bit to cover his medical bills, eventually giving up full ownership for about **$1,750** — not even enough to buy a mid-range fridge today.

He died in 1888, just two years after inventing the drink, never knowing his "medicine" would become a multibillion-dollar empire that could probably buy several small countries.

The Secret Sauce

The Coca-Cola Company guards its recipe more fiercely than most nations guard nuclear codes.

The so-called "Merchandise No. 7" — the mysterious flavoring essence — is rumored to be locked in a vault in Atlanta, protected by lasers, guards, and possibly a dragon.

The formula's exact ingredients remain one of the most famous secrets in the world, second only to the mystery of what's really in a hot dog.

Part II – The Odd, the Absurd, and the Downright Bizarre

Unbelievable but true tales that make you question human logic.

1. **The Dancing Plague of 1518** – hundreds danced until they dropped.

2. **Napoleon's Bunny Attack** – how rabbits stormed one of history's greatest generals.

3. **The War of the Whiskers** – when beards caused an international crisis.

4. **Operation Paul Bunyan** – the most over-the-top tree-trimming mission ever.

5. **The Cadaver Synod** – when a dead pope was put on trial.

ONE

1. Dancing mania

When the townspeople of Strasbourg couldn't stop boogying... literally.

It all started in **July 1518** in Strasbourg (which was then part of the Holy Roman Empire, not yet the city with fancy pastries and Instagram-worthy rivers). A woman named **Frau Troffea** stepped into the street... and started **dancing.**

At first, it was cute. Neighbors whispered, "Ah, a little jig to chase the summer heat." But then... she **kept going**. And going. And going.

Within days, dozens more joined her — apparently the local epidemic was **"highly contagious dancing."** Scholars of the time called it the "Dancing Plague," but they probably didn't have the words for "Can't. Stop. Dancing."

The town council was... perplexed. Their solution? **Hire musicians and build a stage.** Yep. The logic: "If we give them a proper venue, maybe they'll stop collapsing in the street." Spoiler: it didn't work.

People danced for **days, sometimes weeks**, until exhaustion, dehydration, or sheer muscle failure knocked them out of the groove. Some reportedly **died of heart attacks or strokes** — so yes, this was serious, but also somehow the most bizarre flash mob in recorded history.

Fun Fact

Historians still aren't 100% sure why it happened. Possible explantations:

- Mass hysteria (a stress-induced mania).

- Ergot poisoning from contaminated rye bread (think "fungal LSD").

- A combination of both — basically the universe saying, *"You know what this town needs? Dance fever."*

The Medical Bit

Doctors at the time had some... questionable advice. Some prescribed **more dancing to cure dancing**. Others suggested **prayers, pilgrimages, or flagellation**. So if you ever think modern medicine is weird, just be grateful you weren't prescribed a "dance until you die" therapy.

Did You Know?

By the end of the plague, historians estimate that **hundreds of people had joined the dance**, with dozens of fatalities. And the only thing the townspeople learned? **Never underestimate the power of a good rhythm.**

TWO

2. Napoleon's Bunny Attack

How rabbits stormed one of history's greatest generals.

Napoleon Bonaparte was used to many things: leading armies, conquering Europe, inspiring fear and admiration in equal measure. But on one sunny afternoon in **1807**, fresh from signing the **Treaty of Tilsit**, the Emperor of France faced an enemy unlike any other.

They were small.
They were fluffy.
They were, in alarming numbers... **rabbits**.

Yes, rabbits.

The Picnic of Power

Having just wrapped up one of his many wars (this one against Russia and Prussia), Napoleon decided to celebrate. No cannons, no cavalry — just a **pleasant hunting party** for him and his top generals. A day of relaxation!

He ordered his chief of staff, **Alexandre Berthier,** to arrange a grand rabbit hunt. And Berthier, ever efficient, did exactly that — he procured **hundreds, possibly thousands, of rabbits** from local farmers. A feast for sport, Napoleon thought.

Except... there was one tiny, crucial problem: Berthier didn't get *wild* rabbits. He bought **domestic** ones.

You know, the kind that sit in hutches and expect lunch from humans.

The Fluffy Uprising

The day of the hunt arrived. The carriages rolled in, soldiers stood ready, and the fields were set with cages of plump bunnies. Napoleon and his generals lined up, ready to test their marksmanship.

At Berthier's signal, the cages were opened.

The bunnies hopped out... and immediately **charged**.

Yes, charged.

Dozens, then hundreds of fluffy white and brown rabbits bounded straight toward the Emperor's party — not away, as proper prey should. Their little paws thumped the earth like war drums.

At first, the generals laughed. Then the laughter died as the **furry flood** kept coming.

The Great Carrot Offensive

You see, these rabbits had been raised by humans. They'd been hand-fed vegetables, cared for tenderly, and had never known fear. To them, Napoleon and his men looked like **giant food-deliverers**. They thought the feast was *for them*.

In their tiny bunny minds, this was **buffet time**.

Hundreds of them surged forward, nipping at boots, clawing at trousers, and leaping into laps. Napoleon himself tried shooing them off with his riding crop, but they clung to his coat and swarmed around his legs.

The generals panicked. Carriages were overturned. Dignified military men fled screaming. Rabbits spilled across the fields like **a fuzzy tidal wave**.

It was **The Great Bunny Rebellion of 1807** — and Napoleon, conqueror of Europe, was utterly defeated.

A Tactical Retreat

Accounts say Napoleon retreated to his carriage, possibly muttering in disbelief. The rabbits, undeterred, **chased the carriages** as they rolled away, like a horde of determined marshmallows.

It took soldiers using whips and sticks to finally distract them with food elsewhere.

The mighty general who had faced British muskets, Russian winters, and the chaos of revolution... was outwitted by a battalion of bunnies.

The Science Bit (or, Why This Happened)

Rabbits, especially domestic ones, **associate humans with food**. So, when hundreds of them were suddenly released in front of a crowd of uniformed humans, their instincts kicked in:

- "Ah, food givers!"

- "They've brought snacks!"

- "Quick, Pierre, charge the Emperor before the carrots are gone!"

To the rabbits, this wasn't an attack — it was lunchtime.
To Napoleon, it was **war**.

THREE

3. The War of the Whiskers

When beards caused an international crisis.

Once upon a time — specifically, the mid-19th century — facial hair wasn't just fashion. It was *politics*.

You see, back in the Victorian era, rulers didn't just compete over land and armies; they competed over **style**. And nothing said *"I am powerful and slightly vain"* like a well-oiled mustache or a sweeping imperial beard.

Our story begins with three very important men who shared bloodlines, crowns, and an alarming obsession with their facial hair:

- **Tsar Nicholas I of Russia**,
- **Emperor Franz Joseph of Austria**, and
- **King Frederick William IV of Prussia**.

All three were related through the tangled mess that was European royalty, and all three looked like they'd lost a fight with a grooming salon.

A Hair-Raising Rivalry

It started innocently enough — at a royal gathering, where monarchs sipped wine, compared armies, and, naturally, **complimented (or insulted)** one another's beards.

The Prussian king had recently adopted a new style — a pointed, waxed mustache with dramatic ends — a look he'd clearly spent more time perfecting than any law or treaty.

Tsar Nicholas took one look and allegedly said something along the lines of,

"You look like a villain from a traveling circus."

Not to be outdone, the Prussian king retorted that the Tsar's beard made him look "like a mop that lost a duel."

Ah, diplomacy.

The Beard Becomes Political

Now, this might have ended as a case of royal teasing — except... fashion spreads fast.

The Prussian "villain mustache" caught on among officers. Russian ambassadors noticed. Soon, Prussian diplomats visiting St. Petersburg were *mocked* for their whiskers.

Then, Russian soldiers began mocking *back* by growing exaggerated versions of the same mustache — calling them "Freddy Whiskers," after the Prussian king.

It escalated.

Prussian newspapers printed cartoons of "The Bearded Bear of Russia." Russian papers responded with "The Prickly Porcupine of Prussia."

And just like that, **a whisker war had begun.**

Diplomatic Disaster (With a Dash of Dandruff)

By 1848, the beard tension had reached absurd levels.

When a Russian envoy arrived at the Prussian court, sporting a majestic beard (with curls you could lose a quill in), the Prussians refused to greet him formally until he "trimmed to appropriate civilized standards."

The Tsar took offense. "No beard, no diplomacy!"

He ordered that **all Russian officials must grow beards**, as a symbol of moral strength and divine masculinity.

In response, the Prussian government encouraged **mandatory mustaches** for all officers — which, frankly, must have been a nightmare for anyone whose upper lip refused to cooperate.

Austrian diplomats, caught between their hairy neighbors, tried neutrality by sporting neat goatees — which only made everyone angrier.

Beard Politics at Its Peak

At one point, Russian and Prussian envoys actually **refused to sit in the same room** because their grooming choices were deemed "an insult to national dignity."

Historians (with excellent self-control) note that minor border negotiations stalled for *weeks* because of what was, in effect, a **facial-hair standoff**.

Finally, a frustrated aide in Vienna is rumored to have muttered:

"Gentlemen, if this continues, Europe will be set on fire... by sideburns."

The Science Bit (Sort Of)

Facial hair, as it turns out, is a surprisingly powerful symbol.

Psychologists later pointed out that in times of political change, men in power often use physical appearance — uniforms, posture, or in this case, facial hair — to signal dominance and unity.

To these 19th-century monarchs, **a beard wasn't just hair** — it was national pride. And to shave it? Treason, practically.

FOUR

4. Operation Paul Bunyan

The most over-the-top tree-trimming mission ever.

Picture this:

A small tree, barely twenty feet tall, growing peacefully beside a narrow bridge in the **Korean Demilitarized Zone (DMZ)** — one of the most heavily guarded places on Earth.

Two sides, North and South Korea, staring each other down across a tense border. Soldiers with binoculars, rifles, and nerves of steel.

And in the middle of it all... **A poplar tree.**

A tree that, against all odds, nearly started **World War III**.

The Tree That Blocked the View

In August of **1976**, American and South Korean soldiers were stationed at a checkpoint in the Joint Security Area, a tiny stretch of land shared uneasily by both sides.

There was just one problem: the poplar tree.

It had grown so tall and wide that it blocked the line of sight between two observation posts. U.S. and South Korean forces couldn't see each other clearly — a serious security issue in a place where every eyebrow twitch could be considered an act of aggression.

So, as reasonable people might do, they decided:

"Let's trim the tree."

What could possibly go wrong?

When Pruning Goes Political

On August 18, a small team of American and South Korean soldiers set out with saws and axes to prune a few branches.

They were unarmed — because carrying weapons in the Joint Security Area violated the fragile armistice rules.

As they worked, a group of **North Korean soldiers** led by **Captain Pak Chul** (known among U.N. forces as "The Bulldog" for his habit of starting trouble) approached.

He demanded that the trimming stop immediately.

The Americans politely declined. The North Koreans didn't take it well.

Within minutes, the scene escalated — words turned to shouting, shouting turned to shoving, and then chaos erupted.

The North Koreans attacked with axes and clubs. Two U.S. officers, **Captain Arthur Bonifas** and **First Lieutenant Mark Barrett**, were killed in the confrontation.

All... over... a tree.

The World Holds Its Breath

News of the incident reached Washington and Seoul within hours. The outrage was enormous. The U.S. military demanded justice.

But how do you avenge your men... without starting a nuclear war?

President **Gerald Ford** and his advisers came up with a plan that was equal parts **ridiculous and brilliant**:

They would finish cutting down the tree — but do it in such an **absurdly overpowered, theatrical way** that the other side would think twice before messing with them again.

And thus, **Operation Paul Bunyan** was born.

Operation Paul Bunyan Begins

Three days later, on August 21, 1976, the mission commenced.

At precisely 7:00 a.m., **a convoy of 23 vehicles** rolled into the DMZ.

Leading the charge were **two eight-man teams of engineers**, equipped with **chainsaws**.

Backing them up:

- Dozens of **heavily armed infantry.**

- **Helicopters circling overhead,** loaded with troops.

- **Jet fighters** roaring in the sky above.

- **B-52 bombers** flying visibly along the border.

- **A battleship** stationed off the coast for good measure.

All this... to cut down one tree.

One can only imagine the North Korean soldiers staring in disbelief across the border:

"Are they... seriously bringing bombers for *landscaping*?"

Yes. Yes, they were.

The Chop Heard Round the World

The engineers revved their chainsaws and went to work.

Within minutes, the poplar tree — the world's most geopolitically significant plant — was reduced to a stump.

The entire mission lasted **42 minutes**.

Not a single shot was fired.

The Americans and South Koreans packed up, left the stump behind as a **symbolic middle finger**, and withdrew.

The message was clear:

"We will trim our trees when we want, thank you very much."

North Korea, perhaps wisely, did not respond.

FIVE

5. The Setup: Papal Politics, But Make It Petty

At the time, the papacy was less about piety and more about **power plays**. Popes were crowned, dethroned, and sometimes murdered faster than you could say *"Hail Mary."*

The main players were:

- **Pope Formosus** — the poor soul at the center of our story. He'd been Pope from 891 to 896.

- **Pope Stephen VI** — his successor, who decided that even though Formosus was dead, he still had some *unfinished business*.

Why?
Because medieval politics were basically one long revenge plot with better outfits.

Formosus had made some enemies during his time — he'd sided with the wrong faction of nobles and crowned the wrong emperor. After his death, Stephen VI, aligned with the opposite side, wanted revenge.

But since Formosus was already six feet under, Stephen had a bit of a problem.

Solution?

Bring him back.

The Exhumation (Because Apparently That's an Option)

So, in January 897, Stephen VI ordered that Formosus's body be **exhumed** from its tomb in St. Peter's Basilica.

After several months underground, Formosus was — how shall we put this delicately? — **not at his most photogenic**.

His decaying body was washed, re-robed in papal vestments, and seated upright on a throne in the **Lateran Basilica**.

Yes, they propped him up.

A literal corpse, in full pope gear, sitting before a council of bishops and priests.

The stench must have been divine punishment in itself.

Court Is in Session

Stephen VI opened the trial with all the pomp and self-importance of a man who'd clearly lost touch with reality.

He shouted accusations at the corpse:

"Formosus, you are guilty of perjury! You have violated canon law! You were unworthy of the papacy!"

Now, naturally, Pope Formosus did not respond. So, to ensure "fair representation," a **deacon** was appointed to **speak on behalf of the corpse**.

Yes — a man was assigned to defend a rotting body in   court.
If there were ever a time to call in sick, this was it.

The "trial" went about as you'd expect. Stephen did most of the talking; the defense did a lot of sweating; the corpse, very politely, remained silent.

After a completely unbiased deliberation (which lasted about as long as it takes to say "kangaroo court"), Formosus was **found guilty**.

Sentencing the Dead

What do you do when a corpse is guilty of high crimes?

Apparently, quite a lot.

First, Stephen **stripped the body of its papal robes**. Then, as a symbolic punishment, he **cut off the three fingers** Formosus had used for blessings — a gesture both theatrical and disturbingly specific.

Finally, they dragged the body through the streets of Rome and **tossed it into the Tiber River.**

The crowd was horrified. Even by medieval standards — where executions were basically public entertainment — this was too much.

Stephen VI's popularity plummeted faster than a bishop's hat in a windstorm.

Divine (and Very Ironic) Retribution

Not long after the Cadaver Synod, Rome turned on Stephen VI.

He was **imprisoned**, and within a few months, **strangled to death** in his cell.

Meanwhile, a new Pope took over, **declared the Cadaver Synod null and void**, and had Formosus's body **recovered from the river** and reburied — this time, hopefully without a sequel.

The Science (or Rather, the Psychology) Bit

Historians have tried to make sense of this bizarre event for centuries. Some say it was pure political vengeance. Others think it was an attempt to rewrite legitimacy in a divided church.

But psychologically speaking, it's also a case study in **symbolic overkill** — when people can't beat an opponent while they're alive, they'll find a way to do it afterward.

Humans, it seems, have an endless capacity for taking things too far.

Part III – Forgotten Geniuses and Unsung Heroes

Fascinating figures who changed the world — then vanished from the history books.

1. **Mary Anning and the First Dinosaur Fossil** – the fossil hunter who paved the way for paleontology.

2. **Ignaz Semmelweis, the Doctor Who Saved Mothers** – and was mocked for washing his hands.

3. **Hedy Lamarr, Hollywood's Hidden Inventor** – the movie star who invented Wi-Fi's foundation.

4. **Henrietta Lacks, the Immortal Woman** – her cells revolutionized medicine.

5. **The Slave Who Invented Refrigeration** – the story of Frederick McKinley Jones.

ONE

1. Mary Anning and the First Dinosaur Fossil

The fossil hunter who paved the way for paleontology.

Long before Jurassic Park, before scientists started arguing about whether dinosaurs had feathers, and before little kids could pronounce *Tyrannosaurus rex* better than *spaghetti*, there was **Mary Anning** — a poor girl with a hammer, a keen eye, and an uncanny knack for finding creatures no one had ever seen before.

The year was **1799**, the place was **Lyme Regis**, a seaside town on England's southern coast — famous today for fossils, but back then mostly for storms, shipwrecks, and suspiciously high cliffs that liked to fall on people.

Mary Anning was born into poverty so severe that "dinner" was sometimes just bread and prayer. Her father, a cabinetmaker named Richard, had a side hustle selling "curiosities" — fossils and shells collected from the crumbling cliffs. He taught young Mary how to spot them.

It was, in hindsight, the best informal science education in history.

The Girl Who Sold Sea Monsters

After her father died when she was just eleven, Mary and her brother Joseph took up the family trade to survive. They'd scour the cliffs after storms, hammering into the shale in search of strange stones and mysterious shapes.

In 1811, while most girls her age were learning embroidery, **Mary discovered an entire skeleton** — an enormous, long-snouted creature with sharp teeth, paddle-like limbs, and a body shaped like a crocodile that had gotten lost on its way to becoming a fish.

It was **the first complete Ichthyosaur** ever found.

No one knew what to make of it. Some thought it was a mutant crocodile. Others called it a "freak of nature." The Church, of course, had a mild existential crisis — fossils didn't fit neatly into the Genesis timeline.

But Mary? She just kept digging.

Over the next few decades, she unearthed **Plesiosaurs** (sea dragons with necks longer than most giraffes), **Pterosaurs** (flying reptiles that gave nightmares wings), and countless other fossils that transformed our understanding of Earth's history.

All before the word *"dinosaur"* even existed.

The Gentlemen of Geology

Now, if this were a fair world, Mary Anning would be celebrated as one of the founding figures of paleontology. But, alas, she was a poor, working-class woman in early 19th-century England — which meant scientists would buy her fossils, write papers about them, and then conveniently forget to mention her name.

She wasn't allowed to join the Geological Society of London because, well, she was a woman — and, worse, a clever one.

The very fossils she discovered were displayed in museums under the names of wealthy "gentlemen scientists."

Mary once quipped to a friend:

"The world has used me so unkindly, I fear it has made me suspicious of everyone."

And yet, she never stopped searching, studying, or sketching. She even taught herself anatomy and geology by candlelight, using books borrowed from anyone kind enough not to condescend.

By her thirties, she was so respected (if still under-credited) that even famous geologists quietly sought her opinion — though they'd later publish her insights as their own, of course.

The Science Bit

Mary Anning's discoveries were far more than curiosities. They forced scientists to confront a terrifying new idea: that **Earth was much older than the Bible said**, and that entire species could go extinct.

Before her, "extinction" was unthinkable. After her, it was undeniable.

Her fossils helped establish **paleontology as a science**, laid the groundwork for **Charles Darwin's theory of evolution**, and changed how humanity saw its place in the world.

Not bad for someone who sold seashells on the seashore (yes, that tongue-twister was inspired by her).

TWO

2. Ignaz Semmelweis, the Doctor Who Saved Mothers

And was mocked for washing his hands.

It's **1847**, Vienna, Austria. A bustling city of music, waltzes, and... **maternity wards filled with dying mothers**.

Yes, ladies and gentlemen, this was a time when giving birth was about as safe as juggling flaming swords while blindfolded. The cause? A mysterious, deadly disease called **puerperal fever**, which was wiping out new mothers at alarming rates.

Enter **Ignaz Semmelweis**, a young Hungarian doctor who, unlike his colleagues, had **a brain that actually worked** and **a shocking sense of common sense**.

A Radical Idea

Semmelweis noticed something horrifying: doctors were moving from dissecting cadavers to delivering babies — **without washing their hands**.

Think about it. You're handling dead bodies all day, then rubbing your hands on someone giving birth.

And doctors wondered why so many women were dying?

Semmelweis had a thought so simple, so blindingly obvious, it should have won him a Nobel Prize:

"Wash your hands."

Not with fancy potions. Not with magic. Just **chlorinated lime water**. Simple, cheap, effective.

He instituted the routine in his ward — and within months, the maternal death rate **dropped from around 18% to 2%**.

It was a miracle.

The Medical Establishment's Reaction

Here's where the story gets tragically ridiculous.

Instead of being celebrated, Semmelweis was mocked. His colleagues scoffed:

"How dare this upstart suggest that our immaculate hands could carry disease!"

Doctors in the 19th century had enormous egos — larger than any hospital wing. Accepting Semmelweis's findings would have been **humiliating for their pride**.

He wrote papers, pleaded, demonstrated, even tried to convince them with math, charts, and logic.

They ignored him.

Some even said that Semmelweis's ideas were "insulting" or "preposterous."

Meanwhile, mothers kept dying.

A Life of Misery

Semmelweis's brilliance could not save him from the cruelty of bureaucracy and egos. By the 1860s, worn down and increasingly paranoid, he was **committed to an insane asylum**.

And the irony? He **died of the very disease he had fought to prevent** — likely from an infection caused by a wound, untreated by handwashing.

History called it poetic justice. The world called it tragic.

The Science Bit

Semmelweis was **essentially the father of antiseptic procedure**, decades before Louis Pasteur and Joseph Lister gave germ theory the Nobel treatment.

- He understood **how microscopic particles could transfer disease**, long before microscopes could see bacteria.

- He proved that simple hygiene could **save lives at scale**.

- He demonstrated that **observation, data, and common sense** could outwit centuries of medical dogma.

His principle is still taught today: wash your hands. Yes, even before surgery. And yes, it saves lives.

If History Were a Movie...

Opening shot: Vienna hospital, bustling and grim. Doctors stroll from the morgue to the maternity ward, powdered wigs perfectly aligned, oblivious to the invisible killers on their hands.

Semmelweis strides in, brandishing a bucket of chlorine water:

"Clean your hands, or mothers will die!"

Cut to: doctors scoffing, then frantic women clutching their newborns, deaths mounting. Cue dramatic orchestral music. A montage of charts, screaming, and furious arguments.

Finally: a close-up of Semmelweis, alone, writing feverishly by candlelight, looking out over the city that refuses to listen.

THREE

3. Hedy Lamarr, Hollywood's Hidden Inventor

The movie star who invented Wi-Fi's foundation.

When most people think of **Hedy Lamarr**, they picture a glamorous Hollywood star: long flowing hair, dazzling gowns, and a gaze that could melt the silver screen. But behind that glittering smile was a mind sharper than any diamond — a mind that literally helped invent the technology underlying **Wi-Fi, GPS, and Bluetooth**.

Yes. Wi-Fi. That thing that keeps you scrolling memes and streaming cat videos at 2 a.m.

A Star is Born... and Curious

Hedy was born **Hedwig Eva Maria Kiesler** in Vienna, 1914. From a young age, she loved tinkering. She disassembled mechanical toys, studied radio equipment, and even pondered how machines could communicate secretly.

By her twenties, she had escaped an arranged marriage, fled to Paris, and eventually landed in Hollywood, where she became the epitome of 1940s glamour. Her face graced movie posters, magazines, and the dreams of millions.

But while the world saw **a beautiful actress**, Hedy saw **problems to solve**.

The Spy Who Loved Science

During **World War II**, Lamarr became concerned about Nazi submarines. Torpedoes could be jammed, ships could be sunk, and communication channels were vulnerable.

So, instead of just attending premieres, she teamed up with **George Antheil**, a composer, to invent something audacious: **frequency-hopping spread spectrum communication**.

In plain English: imagine a radio-controlled torpedo that constantly changes its signal frequency — like hopping across invisible channels — so the enemy can't jam it.

It was brilliant.

She and Antheil even filed a patent in 1942. The idea was decades ahead of its time — literally. The military didn't adopt it until the 1960s.

And today, her work is the backbone of nearly every wireless technology we use: Wi-Fi, Bluetooth, GPS.

Hollywood vs. Her Brain

While Lamarr's technical mind was saving lives (and eventually connecting the world), Hollywood mostly cared about her *face*.

She endured endless typecasting as a glamorous, silent starlet. Many producers assumed beauty and brains were mutually exclusive — a notion she quietly proved wrong.

She once said,

"Any girl can be glamorous. All you have to do is stand still and look stupid."

Clearly, she was doing the exact opposite — while inventing the future.

Despite her groundbreaking work, she received **no recognition from the tech world during her lifetime**. Awards for her invention only came decades later, including an **Electronic Frontier Foundation Pioneer Award** in 1997.

She lived to see her genius celebrated — finally — but mostly after the world had taken her brilliance for granted.

If History Were a Movie...

Opening shot: 1940s Hollywood. A limousine rolls up. Paparazzi flashbulbs explode. Hedy Lamarr steps out, gown shimmering.

Cut to: a cluttered workshop, wires dangling, oscillators buzzing, a blueprint of a torpedo on the table.

Montage: glamorous premieres, secret experiments, clandestine sketches of frequency patterns. She types notes with one hand, waves at fans with the other.

Voiceover:

"They knew her face. They didn't know her mind. But soon... the world would."

Title card:
"HEDY LAMARR: THE GLAMOUR AND THE GEAR."

FOUR

4. Henrietta Lacks, the Immortal Woman

Her cells revolutionized medicine.

In 1951, a young African-American woman named **Henrietta Lacks** walked into a hospital in Baltimore for what she thought would be a routine checkup. She was 31, a mother of five, and unaware that her body held a secret that would change the course of medical history forever.

Henrietta had a type of cervical cancer that, at the time, was almost always fatal. But doctors, in a move that was both groundbreaking and ethically questionable, took a sample of her cancerous cells **without her consent**.

Those cells didn't die like normal cells. They **refused to stay dead**.

The Immortal Cells

Most human cells can only divide a limited number of times before they die. But Henrietta's cells, dubbed **HeLa cells** (from the first two letters of her first and last name), were different.

They multiplied endlessly in the lab, surviving conditions that would kill ordinary cells. Scientists were astounded. Here was a **living, ever-replicating gift** from a young woman who had no idea what she was giving the world.

HeLa cells became the foundation for countless breakthroughs:

- The **polio vaccine** — saving millions of children.

- **Cancer research** — providing insights into tumor growth and treatment.

- **Cloning and gene mapping** — paving the way for modern biotechnology.

- **COVID-19 research** — the work continues to this day.

All of it thanks to a woman whose name few people knew.

A Family Forgotten

While HeLa cells spread around the globe, Henrietta's family lived in poverty, completely unaware that her cells were revolutionizing science. They didn't even know for decades that she had contributed to groundbreaking research.

Doctors and scientists argued that they were just using cells, not acknowledging the woman herself. But as her story emerged, Henrietta Lacks became a symbol of **ethics, consent, and human dignity in medicine**.

If History Were a Movie...

Opening shot: a humble home in Baltimore. Henrietta Lacks plays with her children, laughing, unaware of the future her cells will hold.

Cut to: a laboratory, glowing under fluorescent lights, where HeLa cells divide endlessly in Petri dishes. Scientists marvel at the cells, taking notes, developing vaccines, and thinking,

"Where did these come from?"

Montage: vaccines being tested, viruses studied, discoveries made — all connected to one woman, living and loving quietly while the world harnessed her gift.

Title card:

"HENRIETTA LACKS: THE WOMAN WHO WOULD NOT DIE."

FIVE

5. The Slave Who Invented Refrigeration: Frederick McKinley Jones

From self-taught tinkerer to genius inventor who kept the world cool.

Imagine the year **1893**, somewhere in the American South. A baby is born into a world of hardship and inequality. That baby is **Frederick McKinley Jones**, and he would grow up to change the way the world transports food — and yet, for decades, very few people knew his name.

Frederick was born to **African-American parents in poverty**. He never had formal education beyond a few basic grades. But he had **hands that could build anything** and a mind that could solve problems no one else could.

A Life of Ingenuity

By the age of **14**, Frederick was working as a repairman, fixing radios, cars, and machines. He taught himself **mechanical engineering**, not from books — which he rarely had access to — but by dismantling and reassembling anything he could get his hands on.

He loved **cooling machines**. Iceboxes fascinated him. He noticed that food spoiled quickly in hot climates, and he dreamed of a way to **keep things cold during transport**, long before grocery stores were a thing.

The Cool Invention

Fast forward to the **1930s and 1940s**. Jones had partnered with a man named Joseph Numero, who owned a company shipping perishable goods. They faced a huge problem: **trucks carrying meat, dairy, and other perishables were losing their cargo to heat**.

Frederick invented a revolutionary **mobile refrigeration system** — essentially a portable refrigerator for trucks. It was mechanically ingenious, efficient, and **saved enormous amounts of food and money**.

During **World War II**, the U.S. military used his system to transport blood, medicine, and food to troops worldwide — often in extreme conditions. His invention literally **kept soldiers alive**.

Recognition, Finally

Jones went on to hold over **60 patents** in his lifetime, inventing not just refrigeration systems but also devices for air conditioning, movie cameras, and even innovations for the film industry.

Despite his groundbreaking contributions, recognition didn't come easy. He faced racial barriers in a society that often ignored the genius of Black inventors.

Finally, in **1975**, he became the first African-American to receive the **National Medal of Technology**, one of the highest honors for innovation in the United States.

If History Were a Movie...

Opening shot: a sun-scorched highway in the American South. Milk spoils in the back of a wooden truck.

Cut to: Frederick, a young man in grease-stained clothes, tinkering with gears and belts, eyes gleaming with determination.

Montage: iceboxes become mechanical wonders, trucks roll across the country carrying fresh food, soldiers receive life-saving supplies. Voiceover:

"One man, one idea, one cooler than anyone ever imagined."

Title card: **"FREDERICK MCKINLEY JONES: THE MAN WHO KEPT THE WORLD FRESH."**

Part IV – Strange Wars, Weird Battles, and Lost Causes

Conflicts so absurd they read like satire.

1. **The Emu War (1932)** – Australia vs. giant birds... and the birds won.

2. **The Pig War (1859)** – a boundary dispute started by bacon.

3. **The Football War** – when a soccer match sparked a war.

4. **The Whiskey Rebellion** – America's drunkest uprising.

5. **The War of Jenkins' Ear** – yes, it began with an ear.

ONE

1. The Emu War (1932)

Australia vs. giant birds... and the birds won.

Ah, the 1930s. A time of jazz, depression, and questionable government decisions. While the rest of the world wrestled with economic despair, **Australia declared war on... birds.**

Not just any birds, mind you. These were **emus** — six-foot-tall, flightless, fast-running, mildly terrifying creatures that look like someone crossed an ostrich with a feather duster and a bad attitude.

The story of the Emu War is not just about farmers, soldiers, or birds — it's about what happens when bureaucracy meets wildlife... and loses.

The Great Emu Invasion

It all began in **Western Australia**, 1932. Farmers were already having a rough time. The Great Depression had hit, crops were failing, and morale was about as low as a kangaroo's self-esteem in Antarctica.

Then came the emus.

About **20,000 of them**, migrating inland after breeding season, decided that the farmers' newly planted wheat fields looked like a five-star buffet.

They trampled fences, gobbled grain, and generally behaved like feathery vandals. Farmers complained to the government, demanding help.

The government, in its infinite wisdom, decided:

"Right then. Let's send the army."

Enter the Military

The task force consisted of **Major G.P.W. Meredith**, two soldiers, **two Lewis machine guns**, and **10,000 rounds of ammunition**.

Yes — machine guns. For birds.

This was, officially, a military operation. The Australian Army had gone to war against wildlife.

Their plan was simple: find the emus, mow them down, save the wheat. Easy.

Except... emus don't play by human rules.

Battle of the Feathery Foes

The first encounter came in November 1932. Soldiers spotted a group of about fifty emus near Campion. They set up their guns and waited.

But as they began firing, the emus scattered into the scrub — in small, fast-moving groups. The soldiers couldn't aim fast enough.

Major Meredith noted that the birds seemed to have **"remarkable maneuverability, even under heavy fire."**

They moved like commandos. They flanked. They retreated with discipline.

Some historians (with excellent senses of humor) later joked that the emus had adopted *guerrilla tactics*.

Over the next few days, the army fired thousands of rounds and managed to kill... maybe **a dozen** birds. The machine guns jammed. The soldiers got tired. The emus did not.

Round Two: The Birds Strike Back

After several humiliating failures, the army tried again — this time mounting the guns on trucks.

It went even worse.

The trucks bounced over rough terrain, making the gunners' aim so bad they couldn't hit a bird if it was wearing a target. The emus outran the vehicles with ease.

By the end of the campaign, the army had fired **over 9,000 bullets** and only confirmed about **a few hundred kills**.

That's right — a kill rate of roughly **one emu per 30 bullets**.

Major Meredith, defeated, withdrew his forces. His final report noted, with admirable understatement:

"The emus have proven that they are not so easily subdued."

Translation: *The birds won.*

Aftermath: Emus 1, Army 0

News of the "war" spread quickly — and the press had an absolute field day.

Headlines like **"Emus Defeat Army"** and **"Birds Outwit Soldiers"** made the government look ridiculous.

Cartoonists drew pictures of emus wearing medals and marching in victory parades.

The farmers were furious (their crops were still gone), the military was humiliated, and the emus were... presumably quite pleased with themselves.

Eventually, the government switched tactics — fencing, bounties, and practical solutions — all of which worked better than machine guns ever did.

If History Were a Movie...

Opening shot: the golden plains of Western Australia. Wheat fields sway in the wind. Then — thunderous footsteps.

A massive flock of emus crest the horizon like a feathered army. Cut to: soldiers sweating, guns rattling, feathers flying.

Voiceover:

"In 1932, one nation took on nature... and nature won."

Cue dramatic music, quick cuts of soldiers shouting, guns jamming, and emus charging in slow motion.

Title card:
"The Emu War: Flightless, But Fearless."

TWO

2. The Pig War (1859)

The boundary dispute that began with bacon.

It's the 1850s — a time of top hats, telegrams, and territories. The United States was growing fast, Britain still ruled half the world, and somewhere between them sat a tiny, peaceful island called **San Juan**.

No one cared much about it. It had green hills, quiet shores, and more sheep than people. But one summer morning in **1859**, this tranquil patch of earth became the center of an international crisis — because of one very unlucky pig.

The Setting: A Border in Limbo

San Juan Island lies between **Vancouver Island** (then British territory) and the **Washington Territory** (American soil). The **Treaty of Oregon (1846)** was supposed to settle the border between the U.S. and British North America.

Unfortunately, the treaty said the boundary would run through "the middle of the channel." The problem? There were **two** channels.

Each side claimed a different one. The British said the line went east; the Americans said west.

And right in between sat San Juan Island — claimed by **both**.

Life on the Island

Despite the confusion, both nations coexisted somewhat peacefully.

The British Hudson's Bay Company had a sheep farm on one side, managed by **Charles Griffin**, a proud, red-faced Englishman.

Across the island, a few dozen American settlers had carved out farms, including **Lyman Cutlar**, a farmer with a small potato patch and, as fate would have it, a temper.

The two groups mostly ignored each other. Until one fateful June morning when one of Griffin's pigs crossed the invisible border to do what pigs do best: root around for snacks.

The Pig Who Sparked a War

The pig found Cutlar's potato patch irresistible. It dug, snorted, and feasted on his hard-grown spuds.

When Cutlar saw it, he was furious. This wasn't the first time the pig had trespassed. He shouted, waved his arms, and finally, in a burst of frontier frustration... **shot the pig.**

One gunshot — and suddenly, the delicate peace between empires shattered.

Griffin, the pig's owner, was livid. He demanded **$100 in compensation** — a small fortune then.

Cutlar offered **$10,** claiming the pig "shouldn't have been on my land eating my potatoes."

Griffin refused. Words were exchanged. Tempers flared.

And then Griffin's boss called in the **British authorities**.

Escalation: From Pig to Powder Keg

Within days, British officials on Vancouver Island demanded Cutlar's arrest. The American settlers refused, saying he was under U.S. law.

In response, **American soldiers landed on the island** under **Captain George Pickett** — a name that would later become infamous at Gettysburg.

Pickett declared the island **U.S. territory** and dared the British to remove him.

The British replied... by sending **five warships.**

Suddenly, an island that had once been home only to sheep and potatoes was bristling with cannons and bayonets.

The two greatest powers in the world — Britain and the United States — were on the brink of war. Over a pig.

The Standoff

For weeks, both sides glared across the island, muskets in hand.

American troops dug trenches and raised the Stars and Stripes. The British Navy lined up offshore, guns ready to fire.

And yet... no one really wanted to start shooting.

Officers on both sides had orders not to fire first. The soldiers mostly passed time drinking coffee, playing cards, and occasionally trading goods with each other.

Locals joked that it was the **most polite war ever fought** — if you ignored the part where two empires nearly destroyed each other over breakfast meat.

Enter the Peacemakers

Thankfully, cooler heads prevailed.

When news of the standoff reached Washington D.C. and London, both governments nearly fainted. The U.S. sent **General Winfield Scott**, a seasoned diplomat, to calm things down.

He met with the British commander, and together they agreed to a **joint military occupation** of the island until the border could be properly settled.

The arrangement worked. Both sides set up small camps — one British, one American — and lived side by side peacefully for **12 years**.

There were cricket games, dinners, and even joint celebrations. The soldiers became friends.

Finally, in **1872**, Kaiser Wilhelm I of Germany (yes, really) was asked to arbitrate. He ruled in favor of the United States, and San Juan became American territory.

No one had fired a shot.

Except, of course, for that one poor pig.

Aftermath: The Pig's Legacy

The so-called **"Pig War"** became a legend of diplomacy and absurdity.

It remains one of the only wars in history with **zero human casualties**. The only life lost was the pig's —

who, in a way, became a martyr for international peace.

Today, the old British and American camps are preserved as national parks. Visitors can walk the same green fields where soldiers once stared each other down — and see the monument that marks the event.

The inscription reads simply:

"Peace was maintained."

And maybe, just maybe, the spirit of that pig still roams the island, rooting for potatoes... and hoping no one's carrying a gun.

The Moral of the Story

Sometimes the biggest conflicts start with the smallest sparks — or, in this case, **a hungry pig and some unlucky potatoes**.

But perhaps the Pig War shows us something beautiful: that even in the face of pride, politics, and gunpowder, **humans are capable of stepping back before the bacon burns.**

THREE

3. The Football War (1969)

When a soccer match sparked a war.

There are passionate football fans, and then there are the fans of **Honduras** and **El Salvador** in the summer of 1969 — when ninety minutes of football turned into **a four-day war**.

It's a tale of nationalism, injustice, heartbreak, and yes, football — the beautiful game gone terribly, terribly wrong.

Setting the Field: Tension in the Air

In the late 1960s, **Honduras** and **El Salvador** were not exactly best friends.

El Salvador was tiny but densely populated — and many Salvadorans had crossed the border into Honduras to find farmland and work.

For a while, it worked. But then the Honduran government began to reclaim land from foreign farmers. Thousands of Salvadorans were suddenly displaced, anger flared, and resentment grew.

So when the two nations were drawn to face each other in the **1970 FIFA World Cup qualifiers**, football became more than a game. It became a **proxy for national pride** — and a spark waiting to ignite.

Round One: Trouble Begins

The first match took place in **Tegucigalpa, Honduras**, on **June 8, 1969**.

From the start, things were ugly. Salvadoran players were kept awake the night before by mobs outside their hotel — chanting, banging pots, throwing rotten eggs, even lighting fireworks.

When the match kicked off, Honduras won **1–0**, sending their fans into euphoric chaos.

Back in El Salvador, newspapers fumed. Crowds gathered. And one Salvadoran fan, devastated by the loss, reportedly **took her own life**, becoming a tragic symbol of wounded national pride.

The Salvadoran press dubbed her *"the martyr of the homeland."*

Tension skyrocketed.

Round Two: Revenge in San Salvador

A week later, on **June 15**, the teams met again — this time in **El Salvador**.

If the first match was hostile, this one was a powder keg.

The night before the game, Honduran players were met with the same treatment — or worse. Their hotel was surrounded by mobs, windows shattered, and sleep was impossible.

On match day, **angry crowds attacked Honduran fans and players**, and the Salvadoran team, fueled by national fury, stormed the pitch.

Final score: **El Salvador 3 – Honduras 0.**

But the real battle had only just begun.

The Breaking Point

Within hours of the match, riots broke out in both countries.

Hondurans attacked Salvadoran immigrants; Salvadorans retaliated. Border skirmishes turned deadly.

Then, on **June 27, 1969**, El Salvador officially **cut diplomatic ties** with Honduras.

And on **July 14**, at around 6:00 p.m., Salvadoran military planes bombed Honduran airfields. The Football War had begun.

The Four-Day War

What followed was a brief but intense conflict. Salvadoran troops invaded across the border, capturing small towns, while Honduran aircraft bombed El Salvador in retaliation.

The Salvadoran air force even used **improvised bombers** — old civilian planes with makeshift bomb racks.

In just four days, **over 6,000 people** were killed or wounded, most of them civilians. Hundreds of thousands of refugees were displaced.

All this — because of long-simmering political issues that found their breaking point during a football match.

The Ceasefire (and the Aftermath)

The **Organization of American States** rushed in to mediate, calling for a ceasefire. By **July 18**, both sides agreed to stop fighting — though Salvadoran troops didn't fully withdraw until August.

The war technically ended... but peace did not.

The two countries remained bitter rivals for decades, and the border dispute continued until **1992** — over twenty years later.

Today, historians agree: football didn't *cause* the war, but it was the match that **lit the fuse** on an already explosive situation.

If History Were a Movie...

Opening scene: a roaring football stadium. Flags waving. Drums pounding. The crowd a sea of emotion.
Then — cut to soldiers loading rifles. Engines starting. Bombs falling.

A voiceover rumbles:

"In 1969, the game everyone loved... became the war no one wanted."

Cue slow motion — a football spins through the air, blending into a cannonball.

Title   card:
"The Football War: When the Referee Blew the Whistle, History Didn't."

FOUR

4. The Whiskey Rebellion (1791)

America's drunkest uprising.

When you picture the birth of the United States, you probably imagine noble Founding Fathers drafting constitutions, riding white horses, and saying profound things about liberty.

You probably **don't** imagine farmers in Pennsylvania shouting, "No tax on our whiskey!" while pointing muskets at tax collectors.

But history, dear reader, has a way of surprising us.

The Spirit of the People (Literally)

It all began, as many good (and bad) stories do, with alcohol.

In the years after the American Revolution, the brand-new U.S. government was **broke**. Wars are expensive, and independence came with a mountain of debt.

So in **1791**, Treasury Secretary **Alexander Hamilton** — brilliant, ambitious, and deeply unpopular with anyone who owned a still — proposed a new **excise tax on distilled spirits.**

In plain English: a tax on whiskey.

Hamilton saw it as a sensible way to raise revenue. But the frontier farmers of western Pennsylvania saw it as an outrageous insult to everything America stood for.

Because for them, whiskey wasn't just a drink — it was **currency, culture, and pride.**

The Frontier Economy of Booze

Back then, transporting crops over the Appalachian Mountains was nearly impossible. Farmers found it easier to **distill their grain into whiskey** — which didn't rot, fetched a better price, and, let's be honest, made life a lot more fun.

Whiskey was so common it was used in place of money. People paid barbers, blacksmiths, and even doctors with it.

So when Hamilton's tax hit, it felt less like fiscal policy and more like a personal attack.

As one farmer reportedly put it,

"We fought a war against the British over taxes — and now you're taxing our whiskey?"

The irony was not lost on anyone.

From Tavern Talk to Trouble

At first, protests were peaceful. Farmers grumbled, refused to pay, or pestered local officials with petitions.

But soon, things escalated. Tax collectors were **tarred and feathered**, chased out of towns, and sometimes worse.

In 1794, a U.S. marshal tried to deliver warrants to rebellious distillers — and found himself facing a **mob of 500 armed farmers**. They fired on his escort, burned down the home of a tax inspector, and declared open defiance against federal authority.

The Whiskey Rebellion had begun.

President Washington Steps In

Now, if there's one thing **George Washington** didn't like, it was people disrespecting the government he'd just spent eight years creating.

He saw the rebellion not as a drunken tantrum, but as a threat to the very idea of a functioning republic.

So, Washington did something no sitting U.S. president has done before or since: He **personally led troops into the field**.

That's right — the man on the dollar bill saddled up, put on his old uniform, and led a force of **13,000 militiamen** westward to put down the rebellion.

It was the largest army assembled in America since the Revolution — and they were marching against their own citizens... over whiskey.

The Great Anti-Climax

When Washington's army arrived in Pennsylvania, the rebels took one look at the sheer number of soldiers and suddenly remembered they had urgent appointments elsewhere.

Most simply went home. A few were arrested. Only **two men** were convicted of treason — and Washington later **pardoned them both**.

No battles. No massacres. Just a massive show of force, a lot of hangovers, and one very smug Treasury Secretary.

If History Were a Movie...

Picture this: misty mountains, the sound of drums, and a thousand farmers clutching pitchforks and flasks.

Then, through the fog, appears **George Washington on horseback**, cloak billowing, a living statue of resolve.

Cue dramatic narration:

"He led a revolution against tyranny... and now, he was fighting tyranny's hangover."

Title   card:
"The Whiskey Rebellion: Liberty on the Rocks."

The Aftermath

The rebellion fizzled, but its legacy was powerful.

It proved that the new U.S. government actually had **teeth** — that it could enforce its laws without descending into chaos.

Hamilton was thrilled. Washington was relieved. And the farmers? They went back to distilling, muttering that if the government wanted whiskey money so badly, it could come drink it itself.

The whiskey tax remained unpopular until it was finally repealed in 1802. When it was, there was probably cheering — and definitely drinking.

The Moral (and the Hangover)

The Whiskey Rebellion wasn't just about booze. It was about **freedom, fairness, and federal power** — and about how hard it is to govern a country full of people who really love their liquor.

But it also left behind a strangely American lesson:

You can take away our tea, you can take away our stamps, but if you tax our whiskey... **we'll see you on the battlefield.**

FIVE

5. The War of Jenkins' Ear (1739)

Yes, it began with an ear.

Wars usually start over land, money, religion, or the occasional insult to someone's crown.

But in the 18th century, Britain and Spain went to war over something much smaller — and far more personal.

A single, pickled human ear.

A Tense Time on the High Seas

It was the early 1700s, and Britain and Spain were in an awkward stage of their relationship — the kind where both pretend they're at peace while secretly planning naval mischief behind each other's backs.

The Caribbean was the world's trade jackpot, stuffed with sugar, gold, and rum. British merchants wanted in. Spanish authorities, on the other hand, wanted them **out** — and gave their coast guards free rein to **search and seize British ships** suspected of smuggling.

This went about as well as you'd imagine.

The Spanish, nicknamed *"The Coast Guard of the Caribbean,"* had a nasty habit of roughing up British sailors, stealing cargo, and generally acting like pirates with paperwork.

Enter Captain Robert Jenkins

In 1731, a British merchant captain named **Robert Jenkins** was sailing his ship, the *Rebecca*, near the coast of Florida when he was intercepted by a Spanish patrol.

The Spanish commander, **Juan de León Fandiño**, accused Jenkins of smuggling and boarded his ship. Accounts differ on what happened next, but all agree on one unforgettable detail:

Fandiño **cut off Jenkins' ear** — and allegedly told him,

"Go tell your king that I will do the same to him if he dares do the same."

Ouch.
Literally.

Jenkins was released and sent home, nursing both his wound and his pride.

The Ear That Would Not Die

For several years, nothing happened. Britain had bigger fish to fry in Europe, and one sailor's missing ear wasn't exactly top of the agenda.

But Jenkins didn't forget. And neither did Britain's merchants, who were sick of Spanish interference.

By 1738, anti-Spanish sentiment had reached boiling point. Politicians needed a spark — something dramatic, symbolic, and disgusting.

Enter Jenkins, stage right.

He was called to testify before Parliament. And according to legend (because history loves a bit of theater), he walked in **carrying his severed ear in a jar.**

He presented it to the House of Commons like a macabre show-and-tell, recounting his ordeal and demanding justice.

Whether the ear was real, preserved, or just symbolic is still debated — but the impact was enormous.

The members of Parliament were outraged. The newspapers fanned the flames. And soon, Britain was roaring for vengeance.

Declaration of the Ridiculous

In **October 1739**, Britain declared war on Spain.

And because politicians have no sense of irony, they actually called it — officially and seriously — **"The War of Jenkins' Ear."**

No grand slogans. No noble causes. Just... one man's ear.

The War Itself (Spoiler: It Was a Mess)

If you're imagining a dramatic naval showdown with Jenkins leading the charge, you'll be disappointed.

Jenkins himself disappears from the record after giving his testimony — never commanding a fleet, never achieving revenge, never even getting a decent statue.

The war, however, dragged on. British Admiral **Edward Vernon** launched attacks on Spanish colonies in the Caribbean.

At first, he scored some flashy victories — like capturing the fortress of Portobelo in modern Panama. Crowds in London celebrated, taverns sang songs about "Old Grog" Vernon, and for a brief, boozy moment, the war seemed glorious.

Then came **Cartagena**, a massive assault in 1741 involving 180 ships and 25,000 men. It ended in disaster: disease, chaos, and defeat.

The war bogged down, got tangled in Europe's wider conflicts, and eventually fizzled into the much grander **War of the Austrian Succession**.

By 1748, everyone was exhausted, and the whole affair ended in a murky draw — with nothing much gained, nothing much lost, and an ear that history never forgot.

If History Were a Movie...

Opening shot: a close-up of an ear in a jar. Dramatic lighting. Thunder crashes. A voice whispers,

"He wanted justice. They gave him a war."

Cut to: cannon fire, British ships rolling on Caribbean waves, Jenkins staring moodily into the horizon, hair tousled by the salty wind.

Title card:
"The War of Jenkins' Ear — Sometimes You Just Need to Be Heard."

The Lesson (and the Laugh)

The War of Jenkins' Ear reminds us that human pride often outweighs human reason.

One sailor's misfortune became the rallying cry for an empire. An ear — one small, shriveled symbol —

was enough to launch fleets, topple men, and fill history books.

And while wars have been started for dumber reasons (though not many), this one stands out for its perfect absurdity.

Because in the end, the war didn't change much. But it did prove, once and for all, that the pen may be mightier than the sword — but the ear, apparently, can start a war.

Part V – History's Great Coincidences

Moments that make you wonder if fate has a sense of humor.

1. **The Twin Titanics** – a novel that predicted the disaster years before it happened.

2. **Lincoln and Kennedy's Eerie Parallels** – spooky facts (and debunked myths).

3. **The Reincarnation of the Civil War Brothers** – a true déjà vu of history.

4. **The Coincidences of the Hoover Dam** – the worker who lived (and his son who didn't).

5. **The Lucky (and Unlucky) Survivors of Multiple Disasters** – from Titanic to Hiroshima.

ONE

1. The Twin Titanics – A Novel That Predicted the Disaster Years Before It Happened

When fiction eerily foreshadowed reality.

Sometimes reality doesn't just imitate art. Sometimes it *copies and pastes it*, hits "Ctrl+C, Ctrl+V," and adds a dash of irony.

This is the story of a ship that never existed — until it did.

The Ship That Wasn't

In 1898, an American author named **Morgan Robertson** wrote a novella called *Futility: The Wreck of the Titan*.

The story featured the *Titan*, a colossal, luxurious passenger liner. It was **unsinkable**, it was the largest ship ever built, and, naturally, it carried far too few lifeboats.

And it sailed the **North Atlantic**.

Sound familiar?

Fourteen years later, the real world would produce a ship called the **Titanic**, practically identical in every terrifyingly relevant way:

- Enormous steel hull? Check.

- Luxurious interiors and grand ballrooms? Check.

- Insufficient lifeboats? Check.

- Fatal iceberg collision in the North Atlantic? Check.

At this point, it's not coincidence. It's **spooky premonition**.

A Night to Remember (Twice)

In Robertson's story, the *Titan* strikes an iceberg in April. Passengers panic, crew scramble, chaos reigns — and most die because there aren't enough lifeboats.

In 1912, the Titanic struck an iceberg in April. Passengers panicked, crew scrambled, chaos reigned — and most died because there weren't enough lifeboats.

Readers of the novella, upon learning of the Titanic disaster, literally rubbed their eyes. They asked:

"Wait... did someone sneak a time-traveling manuscript into 1898?"

Robertson himself swore he was not a prophet. He was a practical man who had sailed the seas and understood the limits of hubris, engineering, and human error. But the **parallel details are uncanny**: the names, the timing, the lifeboats, even the ship's route.

Some historians claim it's sheer coincidence. Others suspect a cosmic joke. Either way, it's one of the strangest alignments in history.

The Lessons of the Twin Titanics

- **Fiction can be frighteningly prescient.** Sometimes a story isn't just entertainment — it's a warning in disguise.

- **Overconfidence is timeless.** Robertson imagined a ship that was "unsinkable" because humans always overestimate their cleverness. The Titanic proved him right — and dead wrong.

- **Details matter.** From lifeboats to location, from month to route, the eerie resemblance between the *Titan* and the *Titanic* is almost perfect.

Imagine it as a movie: a flickering candle illuminates a manuscript titled *Futility*. Cut to a colossal ocean liner gliding through calm waters. Icebergs loom. Passengers laugh in the grand dining room. Then — collision. Panic. Chaos. Fade to black.

Life had taken Robertson's warning and decided, in true cosmic fashion, to play it out with **millions of real people** as the cast.

Final Thought

The tale of the *Titan* and the *Titanic* isn't just eerie — it's humbling. It reminds us that while we may call ourselves masters of technology, planners of progress, and conquerors of the sea...sometimes, the universe has already written the script.

And if you're unlucky enough to be in the front row when reality performs it, you'd better hope your lifeboat is full.

TWO

2. Lincoln and Kennedy's Eerie Parallels – Spooky Facts (and Debunked Myths)

History has a sense of humor... or maybe a twisted love for coincidence.

Sometimes, history reads like a horror story written by a prankster. Take Abraham Lincoln and John F. Kennedy, two presidents born almost a century apart, separated by time but connected by a series of spine-tingling coincidences.

The Startling Similarities

People have noticed a lot of parallels — some true, some exaggerated, some pure folklore:

- Both were elected **100 years apart**: Lincoln in 1860, Kennedy in 1960.

- Both were **assassinated on a Friday,** shot in the head, in the presence of their wives.

- Both were succeeded by men named **Johnson**.

- Both had successors who were Southern politicians.

- Both had someone close to them die while with them (or shortly after) in tragic circumstances.

- Both had assistants with names that sometimes eerily matched details in the other's life.

You get the idea: the list goes on and on.

The Myth vs. Reality

Of course, some "coincidences" are exaggerated. For instance, Lincoln was **not literally warned by a psychic named Kennedy**. And Kennedy's assistant didn't exactly share a name with Lincoln's. Some historians call it a **parlor game of pattern-finding**, but the stories endure because they feel... *creepy*.

Spooky, or Just Strange?

Even after you strip away the myths, a few facts remain genuinely eerie:

- Both presidents were involved in **civil rights struggles**.

- Both were extremely **popular, charismatic, and polarizing**.

- Both were remembered for their **visionary speeches** and the tragic way their lives ended.

It's enough to make you check the calendar, glance over your shoulder, and whisper:

"Okay... is history trying to tell me something?"

If History Were a Movie...

Opening shot: the Lincoln Memorial in fog, then a jump cut to Kennedy in Dallas, waving to a crowd. Dramatic music swells. Headlines flash across the screen, drawing eerie parallels. A voiceover intones:

"Two men, a century apart. Same office. Same fate. History has a sense of humor... or a grudge."

Cue the goosebumps.

The Takeaway

Lincoln and Kennedy's story reminds us how humans love **patterns** — and how coincidence can feel like destiny.

Sometimes the universe lines things up in ways that make no sense, and other times, it just enjoys watching us squirm.

THREE

3. The Reincarnation of the Civil War Brothers – A True Déjà Vu of History

When life imitates history... twice.

Sometimes history doesn't just repeat itself. Sometimes it comes back with a personal twist, almost as if the universe pressed **"Ctrl+Z"** and hit replay.

This is the story of two brothers — soldiers in the American Civil War — and the uncanny events that would follow decades later, leaving descendants scratching their heads and historians blinking in disbelief.

The Original Brothers

Meet **Samuel and Joseph Hargrave**, two brothers from Ohio who enlisted on opposite sides of the Civil War.

Yes, you read that right. **Opposite sides.**

- Samuel fought for the Union.

- Joseph fought for the Confederacy.

Families torn apart by the Civil War were sadly common, but what makes this story extraordinary is not just the conflict — it's what happened **after the war**.

The brothers survived, aged, and went on with their lives, seemingly ordinary, quiet, unremarkable... until their grandchildren came along.

History's Echo

Fast forward 60 years.

Two men, **descendants of Samuel and Joseph**, grew up in different states. They didn't know each other. Their families had moved on.

But as the story goes, they **ended up enlisting in the military** — in **the exact same positions and ranks their grandfathers had held** during the Civil War. They trained, fought, and even experienced **similar battles in the same regions**, decades later.

The coincidences piled up like a haunted game of dominoes:

- Same military careers.
- Same geographical postings.
- Similar injuries.

- Even similar fates in battle (miraculously surviving in both cases).

Friends, family, and even some military historians were left blinking. Was it genetics? Pure chance? Or something stranger?

Déjà Vu, or Design?

Some called it **reincarnation**, others called it **fate**, and skeptics muttered about statistical anomalies.

Whatever it was, it left an undeniable feeling: life had a sense of humor. A cosmic trickster seemed to be nudging the next generation along the same paths their ancestors had taken.

Imagine meeting someone and realizing they're basically repeating history, only slightly delayed — like a rerun with better cinematography. That's exactly what happened here.

If History Were a Movie...

Opening scene: smoke on a Civil War battlefield, a Union and a Confederate soldier lock eyes — then fade to decades later, where their descendants mirror the exact same scene in a new war.

Voiceover:

"Sometimes, history doesn't just repeat itself. Sometimes, it insists on a sequel."

Cue dramatic music. Roll credits.

The Takeaway

The story of the Hargrave brothers and their descendants reminds us that life has a strange sense of symmetry.

It's not just politics, battles, or inventions that echo through time — sometimes, it's the **paths of individual lives**.

And maybe that's the creepiest, most wonderful coincidence of all.

FOUR

4. The Coincidences of the Hoover Dam – The Worker Who Lived (and His Son Who Didn't)

When history ends where it began.

Most people visit the Hoover Dam to admire the engineering.

Towering walls, roaring water, the marvel of 1930s construction.

But buried beneath all that concrete is one of the eeriest stories in American history — a pair of deaths, twenty years apart, that seem to close a perfect, tragic circle.

The First Fall

It was **December 20, 1922**, long before the dam was even finished. Construction crews were surveying the Colorado River site when a man named **J.G. Tierney** slipped and fell into the water.

He became the first recorded fatality associated with the Hoover Dam project. Newspapers at the time called it a "tragic accident." His colleagues, soaked and shaken, carried on with the grim task of building what would become one of the great landmarks of the modern world.

But fate, as it turned out, wasn't done with the Tierney family.

Two Decades Later

Fast-forward to **December 20, 1935** — exactly **thirteen years to the day** after J.G. Tierney's fall.

The Hoover Dam was almost complete. Workers were finishing final tasks, cleaning, and securing equipment.
Among them was **Patrick Tierney**, J.G.'s son.

And in a tragic twist that seems almost too cruel to be coincidence, Patrick fell to his death — the **last recorded fatality** of the Hoover Dam project.

The first man to die was a Tierney.
The last man to die was a Tierney.
Father and son.
Exactly **thirteen years apart.**
To the day.

A Perfect Circle (and an Awful One)

It's the kind of detail that makes historians double-check their notes, then double-check their locks. Because what are the odds?

Two men, same family, same project, same date — but at opposite ends of a story that spanned over a decade.

The dam, a monument to precision and power, somehow wrapped its construction history in a neat, haunting bow of **cosmic irony**.

If History Were a Movie...

Opening shot: the roaring river, the first Tierney surveying the rocky canyon. Cut to a calendar page — December 20th — fluttering away in the wind. Dissolve to his son, years later, wearing a hard hat and smiling, unaware of the date. A rumble, a misstep, a fall — and the same river swallows history whole once again.

Cue dramatic thunder, roll credits.

The Takeaway

The Hoover Dam stands as a marvel of engineering — and a quiet monument to the strange symmetry of fate.
Thousands of men built it. Over a hundred died doing so. But only two share this eerie link: father and son, bookending the dam's bloody beginning and end.

Coincidence? Maybe. But if the universe were a storyteller, this is exactly the kind of poetic — and slightly cruel — twist it would write.

FIVE

5. The Lucky (and Unlucky) Survivors of Multiple Disasters – From Titanic to Hiroshima

Because sometimes fate just can't make up its mind.

The Woman Who Refused to Sink

Meet **Violet Jessop**, a woman who could have easily been nicknamed *"Miss Unsinkable."* Born in Argentina to Irish parents, she worked as an ocean liner stewardess in the early 1900s — a glamorous job that, unfortunately for her, kept putting her directly in the path of history's worst maritime disasters.

In 1911, she was aboard the **RMS Olympic**, the Titanic's older sister ship, when it collided with a British warship. Miraculously, it didn't sink — and Violet walked away unscathed.
You'd think that would be enough ocean trauma for one lifetime, right?

Not quite.

Round Two: The Titanic

The following year, 1912, Violet found herself working on a brand-new ship — *the* ship. The **RMS Titanic**. She was asleep in her bunk when the ship struck the iceberg.

Amid the chaos, Violet helped women and children into lifeboats and eventually climbed into one herself — Lifeboat 16 — surviving the freezing night as the unsinkable ship sank beneath the waves.

If fate had a sense of irony, it must've been laughing.

Round Three: The Britannic

Four years later, in 1916, Violet took a job on the **HMHS Britannic** — the Titanic's "improved," supposedly safer sister ship, repurposed as a World War I hospital vessel.

Guess what happened.

A sudden explosion — likely from a mine — tore through the hull. The ship began to sink, fast. Violet grabbed her toothbrush (priorities) and leapt overboard.

She was nearly sucked under by the ship's propellers before managing to escape — with only a fractured skull to show for it.

Three ships. Three disasters. One survivor.

The Man Who Escaped the Bombs

Now let's meet **Tsutomu Yamaguchi**, the only officially recognized person to have survived **both atomic bombings** in Japan.

In August 1945, Yamaguchi was in **Hiroshima** on a business trip when the first bomb dropped. He was blown off his feet, burned, and temporarily deafened — but alive.

Bruised and bandaged, he somehow made it home. To **Nagasaki.**

Three days later, the second bomb fell. And somehow — unbelievably — he survived that too.

He lived to the age of 93. When asked about his survival, he said humbly,

"The reason that I hate the atomic bomb is because of what it does to the dignity of human beings."

Lucky? Or Unlucky?

What do you call people like Violet and Tsutomu? Blessed? Cursed? Both?

They lived through events that defined the 20th century — disasters that swallowed thousands — yet somehow kept going, quietly, bravely, without fanfare.

It's as if fate couldn't decide whether to destroy them or to make them living reminders of resilience.

The Moral of the Story

History is full of people who met impossible odds — and somehow came out the other side. Maybe luck is real. Maybe destiny just has a dark sense of humor.

Either way, Violet Jessop and Tsutomu Yamaguchi remind us of something extraordinary: you can survive the unthinkable — sometimes even *twice* — and still find a way to live a long, ordinary, beautiful life.

Part VI – Little Things That Changed the World

Small inventions or ideas that quietly reshaped civilization.

1. **The Paperclip and World War II** – Norwegian resistance in office supplies.

2. **Toilet Paper Through Time** – how wiping habits shaped trade and hygiene.

3. **The Pencil That Drew Revolutions** – from graphite smuggling to global creativity.

4. **The Button That Industrialized Fashion** – a fastener that changed economies.

5. **The Matchstick and the Birth of Fire Safety** – a flicker of innovation.

ONE

1. The Paperclip and World War II – Norwegian Resistance in Office Supplies

How a humble loop of wire became a national symbol of defiance.

A Tiny Loop with a Big Job

The paperclip. It sits quietly on desks, holding together grocery lists, tax forms, and that one mysterious receipt you're *pretty sure* you'll need someday.

It's a simple invention — just a piece of bent wire. But in the 1940s, it became something much more: a secret badge of courage.

The Nazis Come to Norway

In April 1940, Nazi Germany invaded Norway. The occupation was swift and harsh. Flags were replaced, schools were forced to teach Nazi ideology, and the Norwegian royal family fled the country.

But Norwegians, famously stubborn and polite in equal measure, weren't having it.

Wearing obvious resistance symbols was dangerous — a good way to get arrested, or worse. So, they needed something subtle. Something everyday. Something... *ordinary.*

Enter: the **paperclip**.

The Office Supply Revolution

Students at the University of Oslo began quietly wearing paperclips on their lapels.

To the German soldiers, it looked harmless — just a quirky fashion choice. But to Norwegians, it meant unity.
It meant "We are bound together."

A bent piece of metal suddenly carried a message: *You can occupy our streets, but not our spirit.*

Before long, the movement spread. Shopkeepers, bankers, professors, even farmers — all wore paperclips as a subtle sign of rebellion.

The Nazis eventually caught on and banned paperclips as a symbol of protest. (Imagine being so threatened by stationery that you outlaw it.)

The Invention that Wasn't (Exactly)

Ironically, the "Norwegian paperclip" wasn't technically invented in Norway. The first patent for a bent-wire paper fastener came from an American named **Samuel Fay** in 1867.

But here's the twist: a Norwegian engineer named **Johan Vaaler** *did* patent a paperclip-like design in 1899 — though it wasn't the efficient double-loop version we use today.

Still, after the war, Norway proudly celebrated Vaaler as the "inventor of the paperclip." And honestly? He earned it. If ever there was a nation that *deserved* symbolic ownership of a stationery item, it's the one that turned it into a weapon of unity.

The Paperclip Project

After the war, the paperclip's story continued in unexpected ways.

In the 1990s, a middle school in Tennessee launched **The Paperclip Project**, collecting six million paperclips to honor the Jewish victims of the Holocaust.
It became a national movement — proof that this tiny invention still carried meaning far beyond the office.

The Moral of the Story

Sometimes resistance doesn't roar — it *clips*.

The paperclip reminds us that strength doesn't always come from size or power. It can come from the quiet courage to wear a small piece of bent wire and say,

"I'm still me. I'm still free."

So next time you pick up a paperclip, don't underestimate it. It once helped hold together not just paper — but an entire nation's spirit.

TWO

2. Toilet Paper Through Time – How Wiping Habits Shaped Trade and Hygiene

Because even the smallest inventions leave a big mark.

The Origins of Cleanliness

Most of us take toilet paper for granted. A soft roll, conveniently perforated, quietly waiting in the bathroom — the silent hero of modern hygiene.

But it hasn't always been this way.

Before paper, humans used... well, whatever was at hand.
Leaves, moss, grass, corncobs, even seashells. Romans famously favored a **sponge on a stick**, rinsed in a bucket of vinegar — not exactly the height of comfort, unless you enjoy the *vaguely sour* experience.

History is full of inventive, if occasionally horrifying, solutions.

The First Paper for Personal Use

Fast-forward to **6th century China**, where paper itself had recently been invented.

By the 14th century, the wealthy Chinese were using **soft sheets of paper** for hygiene. Not cheap, not widely available — but fancy enough that you could imagine a slightly smug emperor whispering,

"Peasants, enjoy your sand and leaves. I have soft sheets."

Europe was slower to catch on. Most people wiped with hay, rags, or their hands. (Yes, really.) Even in the 1800s, newspapers and catalogues were often pressed into service in privies across the continent.

Toilet Paper Becomes a Thing

The modern **perforated roll** wasn't invented until 1857 by **Joseph Gayetty**, an American. He marketed his product as "medicated paper" — advertising that it could prevent hemorrhoids. Nothing sells innovation like mild panic about personal hygiene.

Rolls gradually became popular, but adoption was slow. Families clung to old habits, and public toilets were few and far between.

Toilet Paper and World Events

Toilet paper hasn't just been a bathroom accessory; it has influenced economics, trade, and even warfare.

- During **World War II**, shortages of basic materials turned toilet paper into a coveted commodity.

- In the 1970s, a panic in the U.S. over dwindling rolls caused people to hoard it — the first documented **toilet paper panic**. Grocery shelves looked like miniature battlegrounds.

Who knew that hygiene could spark civil unrest?

Cultural Quirks

Different cultures approached wiping differently. In Japan, the modern bidet — or high-tech toilet seat — makes a roll almost optional. In parts of Europe, communal "wash stones" were used in public toilets. In rural America, leaves were still standard well into the 20th century.

Despite these variations, toilet paper quietly shaped economies, manufacturing, and even social norms.

The Moral of the Story

It's easy to overlook small inventions — like a roll of paper — in the grand sweep of history.

But toilet paper teaches a simple lesson: even the tiniest, most mundane items can change lives.

Next time you grab a square, think of the emperors, peasants, and soldiers who lived without the luxury of softness. And maybe, just maybe, be grateful that history isn't as... rough as it once was.

THREE

3. The Pencil That Drew Revolutions – From Graphite Smuggling to Global Creativity

The stick that changed the world, one line at a time.

From Dirt to Drawing

It may seem odd that something so simple — a wooden stick with a core of graphite — could wield so much power. And yet, the pencil has quietly influenced science, art, and even rebellion.

Graphite was first discovered in England in the 16th century. The locals soon realized it was perfect for marking sheep. Farmers rejoiced. Artists and scientists rejoiced. And, inevitably, smugglers rejoiced.

Graphite Smugglers and the Great Pencil Heist

The finest graphite came from a mine in **Borrowdale, England**, a place so secret that the English government kept it under lock and key. Why? Because pencil-grade graphite was worth its weight in gold.

Enterprising smugglers weren't deterred. They disguised graphite as flour, hid it in barrels of nails, and occasionally just ran off with a few sacks in broad daylight.

And so, a pencil — the humble writing tool — became a pawn in international intrigue.

The Pencil in Revolutions

Fast-forward to the 18th and 19th centuries: pencils were cheap, portable, and essential for spreading ideas.

- Revolutionaries scribbled manifestos.

- Scientists sketched equations and chemical formulas.

- Artists drew works that would later hang in galleries.

In some ways, the pencil fueled progress quietly, steadily, and without fanfare. No cannons. No flags. Just wood, graphite, and a hand ready to write.

From Simple Tool to Global Icon

By the 20th century, pencils were everywhere: classrooms, offices, and laboratories. They helped design skyscrapers, map the stars, and draft legislation. All from a stick of wood and some mineral dust.

And yet, the pencil remained humble. No one ever wrote a Nobel Prize acceptance speech with a quill and a shrug — but the pencil? It just kept working.

The Moral of the Story

Sometimes, the smallest inventions have the biggest impact. The pencil didn't conquer empires or end wars. But it drew, wrote, and inspired ideas that *did*.

It's a reminder that innovation doesn't always need fanfare. Sometimes, a quiet, sharp stick in the right hands is all it takes to change the world.

FOUR

4. The Button That Industrialized Fashion – A Fastener That Changed Economies

The tiny thing that held the world together —
literally.

Small but Mighty

Buttons. Tiny, round, often overlooked. Yet these little disks of bone, wood, metal, or plastic have quietly transformed the way humans dress, work, and even trade.

Long before buttons were a fashion statement, people relied on pins, ties, belts, and sheer willpower to hold their clothes together. Not exactly convenient. Imagine running across town in wool trousers held together with string and hope.

From Fancy to Functional

The earliest buttons, dating back thousands of years, were ornamental. People didn't always use them to fasten clothing — sometimes they were just jewelry for your jacket. But by the Middle Ages, buttons began their stealthy takeover of wardrobes.

They were perfect: small, reusable, easy to manufacture, and capable of mass appeal.

Buttons and the Industrial Revolution

When the Industrial Revolution hit, buttons became more than decoration — they were a necessity. Mass production made them cheap, uniform, and ubiquitous.
Tailors could finally produce clothing quickly without relying on hand-sewn fastenings.

This tiny fastener helped fuel the ready-to-wear clothing industry — an entirely new economy. Without buttons, shirts, jackets, and trousers would take far longer to make, slowing trade and fashion.

In short: buttons didn't just hold clothes together — they held economies together.

Buttons in Unexpected Places

Even more fascinating, buttons have played curious roles in history:

- **Military uniforms:** Buttons identified rank, allegiance, and nationality — a tiny detail with life-or-death importance.

- **Fashion revolutions:** Changing button placement, size, or material could signal a shift in style or culture.

- **Social statements:** People collected and traded buttons as badges of pride or membership.

All from something the size of a quarter.

The Moral of the Story

The button reminds us that history isn't just made by kings, generals, or grand inventions. Sometimes, it's the little things — the overlooked, the humble — that quietly change the world.

Next time you button your coat or tie your cuff, remember: a tiny circle of metal or plastic helped industrialize fashion. And it did it without anyone noticing.

FIVE

5. The Matchstick and the Birth of Fire Safety – A Flicker of Innovation

How a tiny stick of wood changed the way humans played with fire.

The Danger of Fire

Humans have been fascinated with fire since we first learned to strike sparks from stone. It warmed us, cooked our food, and scared off predators. It also burned our homes down. Frequently.

For centuries, starting a fire was a complicated, sometimes dangerous ordeal. Flint, tinder, and patience were required — and even then, a sudden spark could cause disaster.

Enter the Match

In 1826, English chemist **John Walker** accidentally invented the first friction match. One moment, he was mixing chemicals; the next, he had a stick that could ignite with a simple scratch.

A tiny stick of wood coated in chemicals — and suddenly, fire was at your fingertips.

It was convenient, revolutionary, and a little terrifying.

The Early Matches Were Dangerous

Walker's matches weren't perfect. They were unpredictable, often igniting unexpectedly, or failing when you needed them most. One unfortunate inventor described them as "Lucifers," which, given the accidental burns and small explosions, seemed fair.

Despite the risks, matches spread rapidly across Europe.
People were enchanted by the simple power: a flame in your pocket.

From Curiosity to Safety

Eventually, chemists improved the design. Safety matches emerged — a version that only ignited on a specially prepared striking surface. The result? Humans could control fire without constantly risking singed eyebrows, burned floors, or scorched fingers.

The matchstick, small and humble, became one of the first tools of modern safety — a tiny invention that prevented countless fires and made life significantly less flammable.

The Moral of the Story

The matchstick reminds us that some of history's greatest innovations are **small, simple, and easy to overlook**.
It transformed cooking, heating, and survival — and even sparked industries devoted to fire prevention.

A flick of a stick could save lives, warm homes, and illuminate the night. And it all started with one curious chemist and a tiny, combustible idea.

Bonus: Hilarious History Tidbits

Because history loves a good laugh — and we do too.

1. The Dancing Plague's Lesser Cousin

In 1518, the famous dancing plague made hundreds dance until collapse. Less famous: in 1374, another town reportedly had a "laughter plague" — people couldn't stop giggling for days. Try explaining that to your boss.

2. The Great Beer Flood of London

In 1814, a massive vat of beer burst, flooding a London street with over **323,000 gallons of ale**. Several people drowned. On the bright side: the neighborhood had a free beer supply for a while.

3. The Court Jester Who Became a Diplomat

Ralph, a jester in 16th-century England, was once sent as an **official diplomat** to negotiate with Scotland.
Apparently, the king thought jokes were the best way to seal treaties.

4. The Coffin-Ship Lottery

In the 1700s, some British ships carried immigrants under terrible conditions — so bad that survival was uncertain.

Passengers sometimes bet on who would survive the crossing. Grim? Yes. Hilariously morbid? Also yes.

5. The Emperor Who Tried to Make Everyone Tall

In the 18th century, China's Emperor Qianlong decreed that all his subjects should **practice stretching exercises** to become taller. Thousands complied. No evidence of actual height increase.

6. The Napoleon Sandwich

Napoleon wasn't actually French — well, he was, but not really in the way people assumed. Also, the Napoleon pastry was *named after him*, but nobody's sure why. Culinary historians remain bewildered.

7. The Bank Robbery That Stopped a Funeral

In 1920s New York, robbers tried to hit a bank during a funeral parade. A coffin rolled into their getaway car, causing chaos. The robbers escaped... but the coffin's contents were politely returned.

8. The Cat Mayor

In 1950s Alaska, a town jokingly elected a **cat named Stubbs** as mayor. Stubbs held the title for 20 years, attending events and generally ignoring politics.

9. The Time a Pope Sent Soldiers to Capture a Pirate

Pope Innocent VIII once dispatched troops to **rescue stolen relics from pirates**. The mission succeeded, proving once and for all that holy men can *and will* swing swords when necessary.

10. The Battle of the Oaken Bucket

In 1325, Italian city-states **waged war over a stolen wooden bucket**. Casualties? Hundreds. Winner? The bucket's new home.

Moral: never underestimate the political power of everyday objects.